Skyscrapers
A Project Book

To Ma, Pa, and the Big Apple

Skyscrapers: A Project Book
is designed to encourage
children to participate in
the learning experience–to learn by
practical example. *Skyscrapers*
traces the history of these
superstructures up to the present
day. Through its pages it leads the
reader to the construction of a model
skyscraper, element by element.
Simple instructions, clearly
illustrated, are included and as far
as possible are based on real
architectural and engineering
principles. The materials called for
should be readily available,
inexpensive, and safe to use.
Technical terms, translated
into layman's language, make this
book interesting reading for
children and parents alike.

Skyscrapers

A Project Book

Anne and Scott MacGregor

Lothrop, Lee & Shepard Books • New York

The authors wish to thank the following
organizations for their assistance with
information and materials: Cement and
Concrete Association; Citibank N.A.;
The Empire State Building Company;
The Otis Elevator Company; The Port
Authority of New York and
New Jersey; National Westminster
Bank Ltd.

Designed by Nick Thirkell,
assisted by Ian Loveday.

Library of Congress Cataloging in Publication Data
MacGregor, Anne, (date)
Skyscrapers.
SUMMARY: A history of skyscrapers from the
first century to the present and a description
of their construction and services. Includes
instructions for making a model skyscraper
complete with elevator.   1. Skyscrapers—Juvenile
literature. [1. Skyscrapers]   I. MacGregor, Scott,
(date) joint author.   II. Title.
TH1615.M33   721'.042   81-342   AACR1
ISBN 0-688-00368-0 (lib. bdg.)
ISBN 0-688-00365-6 (pbk.)

Contents

I Skyscrapers: the Beginning

Skyscrapers have become a familiar sight in twentieth-century cities. They were first built about one hundred years ago to solve a problem faced by cities throughout the world–namely, too many people sharing too little land. While skyscrapers have succeeded in solving one problem by accommodating thousands of people within four or more very tall walls, they have created other problems.

In some cities, skyscrapers have grown so tall and close together that it's difficult to see the sky. Life on the ground, therefore, around skyscrapers, is sometimes very unpleasant.

Also, skyscrapers may well be called "energy vultures," because of the alarming way they eat up natural resources like oil and gas to keep themselves running. When the world's supply of these resources is used up, however, it won't matter how many people a skyscraper can hold, because without natural resources, life as the world knows it will not be quite the same.

Fortunately, some people who build skyscrapers now realize how bleak the future will be if energy resources continue to be wasted. Systems are being developed today that *conserve*, or save, energy.

In any case, skyscrapers are fascinating buildings and for this reason it is worthwhile trying to understand them. To do this, it is necessary to follow their development, beginning with the first multistory shelters.

Multistory Caves

Pictured here is a multistory cave in Cappadocia in Turkey. Nature was the architect of these dwellings, which were inhabited from the first century until 1924. Wind and water first carved the caves from tufa stone hills. (Tufa is compacted volcanic dust, which settled in this region following eruptions of the Erciyas volcano.) Later, residents added rooms, doorways, windows, and stairways by wetting the stone and carving out openings, using basic tools. As the population of these caves increased, more living space was created, and like the modern skyscraper the direction these extensions took was up–sometimes as high as sixteen stories.

8

Roman Apartment Houses

During the first century A.D., multistory apartment blocks appeared in the Italian port of Ostia and the capital, Rome. Both cities had large populations. Land was in short supply, and only the rich could afford to live in individual *domus*, or houses. *Insulae*, six- and seven-story houses made of timber, concrete, and brick, were built to accommodate great numbers of people on the limited amount of land that was available in these cities.

Tabernae, or shops, workshops, and taverns, were located on the insulae's ground floor, just like the street-level shops being included in many modern skyscrapers. This arrangement provided Roman families with shopping and entertainment facilities nearby and this, in turn, helped to establish self-sufficient, close-knit communities. Shopping plazas in today's skyscrapers are meant to do the same thing. Balconies surrounding the insulae provided walkways to the rooms. Wooden shutters covered window openings, as glass was not yet made in large enough quantities for this purpose. Windows faced out on narrow streets, so residents had very little privacy and almost no protection from noise outside, or indeed from apartments just next door. But windows let natural light and fresh air into the insulae's small rooms; they were also used as an outlet for household rubbish, since the streets were the common disposal areas.

Besides poor rubbish disposal facilities, there were other risks to health and safety at that time from lack of plumbing, cooking, and heating facilities. The Romans had not yet worked out a way to pump water to upper floors of the insulae, so residents had to use street fountains and public baths and toilets. Wood-burning stoves provided the only form of heating and were also used for cooking. Under these conditions, fire could easily happen and, without a ready supply of water, there were no means to extinguish it or prevent it from spreading to nearby buildings. Indeed, the fire of A.D.64, which destroyed most of Rome, forced builders to make changes to insulae to avoid another catastrophe.

The maximum size of a multistory building was fixed at 21.5m (70 ft). Mud brick was to be replaced by concrete; the use of timber was to be limited. All new insulae were required to have their own separate walls. (Previously, apartment blocks shared what is known as a *party* wall, which helped fires to spread quickly.)

9

The European region enjoyed a period of relative peace beginning with the eleventh century, during which time buildings rose to even greater heights. Roman garrisons that had previously protected the Empire were closed, and the armies were withdrawn. Without this security, wealthy families built their own defensive towers to protect themselves against possible attack by foreign invaders. Since there was also great rivalry within their own communities, noble families built towers to defend themselves against each other.

Villages like Svanetia in the Caucasus Mountains put a great deal of energy into the construction of defensive towers. So many towers were built at that time, each attempting to gain a height advantage over the other, that village skylines soon resembled a small-scale version of today's cities.

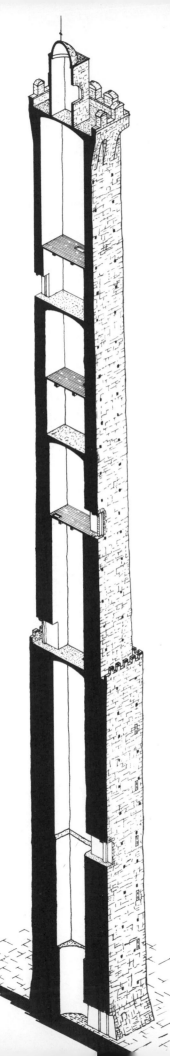

Defensive Towers

Towers were simple in design and solid looking. They were made of bricks and marble–materials that were easily found. Bricks were small and tightly packed, with thick layers of mortar in between the *courses,* or rows. Window openings from which to fire weapons were narrow–just big enough to let in fresh air and light.

Pictured here is a cutaway of the Torre Asinelli, which was built in Bologna, Italy, in 1109. Such towers were built as high as 100m (325 ft). Observation decks were perched at the top, and sometimes midway down the building.

Though these were temporary shelters, there were living spaces and large rooms for the storage of food, water, and ammunition. Towers also had fireplaces, which could be used for heating and cooking.

To support so great a weight, a tower's walls needed to be as thick as possible at the base, where the greatest weight rested and therefore the most strength was required. As a result, the space available on the lower floors was very limited indeed.

Foundations proved to be insufficient to support such tall buildings, so that many of these sank, tilting under their own great weight.

II Foundations: from the Bottom Up

The first problems to be solved in skyscraper construction were obvious as far back as the Middle Ages. If multistory houses, cathedrals, and public buildings were to be constructed on a grand scale, improvements would have to be made to foundations so that they would be strong enough to support great weights on any type of soil.

The foundation is the base on which a building rests its full weight, as well as the added weight caused by wind pressure. It is in direct contact with the ground and should be strong enough to carry the building's weight as evenly as possible.

The earth is made up of different layers of soil, which are pressed in a downward direction under a building. This is known as *settlement*. Unfortunately, particles of soil may be more easily compressed in some areas than in others. When this happens, the foundation and the building it supports may sink unevenly, causing cracks and other damage throughout the building.

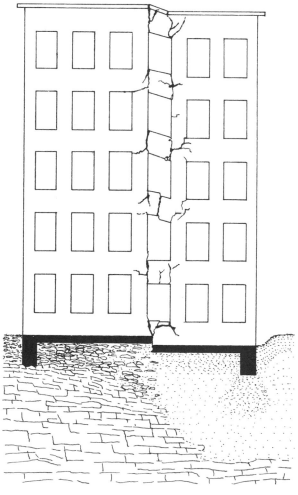

The first step in building a skyscraper is a *site survey*, which is a thorough study of all features of the ground: what makes up the layers of the earth; the moisture contained in the soil that results from underground waterways; and any movements that are likely to happen because of earthquakes and other forces of nature.

Two Kinds of Foundations

Skyscrapers may have either deep or shallow foundations. These are the two, broad classifications, and the type used depends on what the ground, or *foundation bed*, is made of.

Piles are used for deep foundations, when the ground near the surface is soft. Piles can be driven into the foundation bed by using mechanical *pile drivers*, or they can be built in place. In the latter case, holes are drilled into the ground and filled with concrete, which is *reinforced*—made stronger by the addition of steel rods.

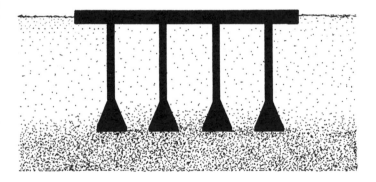

Spread footings may be used at the ends of the piles. They have a wide base that looks like a foot, and they carry weight over a larger surface area to fix this type of foundation in place.

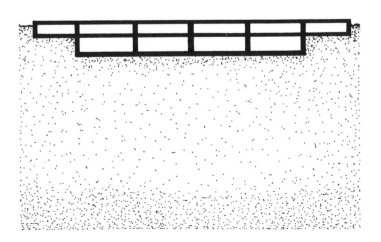

Raft foundations, which are classified as a shallow type, are those that support an entire building in one continuous piece. These foundations work in the same way as a raft or flat-bottomed boat–that is, they float on a sea of earth, spreading a building's weight over the maximum area. Rafts are used when there is no solid soil at a reasonable depth in the foundation bed. They are usually built of reinforced concrete. In recent years, however, steel grilles have been used to do the job.

These foundation types are not new; they have been used for hundreds of years. Spread footings support some of the great cathedrals built in the fifteenth century. Until the nineteenth century few changes were made to these methods except in the manner in which they were put into the ground. Only when the first modern skyscrapers were being built did architects, engineers, and builders search for new methods of constructing foundations that would support buildings of more than twenty stories.

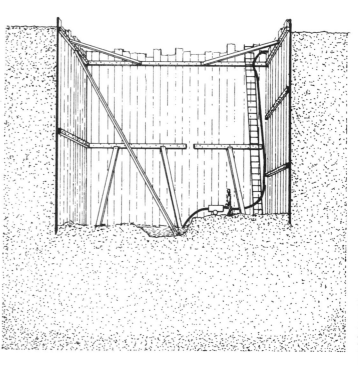

The deeper a skyscraper's foundation is placed, the more likelihood there is of finding water in the foundation bed. Naturally, this made it far more difficult to work in an area. The same problem existed in bridge building, however, and in that industry led to the invention of *cofferdams*, or dry working chambers. Cofferdams were first used by the Romans, who built theirs out of wood, packed with mud. Today, cofferdams are framed in wood in which reinforced concrete is cast. As pictured, water is pumped out of a cofferdam so that men can work comfortably in a dry space.

Modern foundations sometimes use what is known as the *buoyancy principle*. This is done by excavating the foundation bed and removing an amount of earth equal in weight to the building itself, which provides enough support. The resulting space created under the building is used for basements, which can provide storage space for machinery or parking spaces for vehicles.

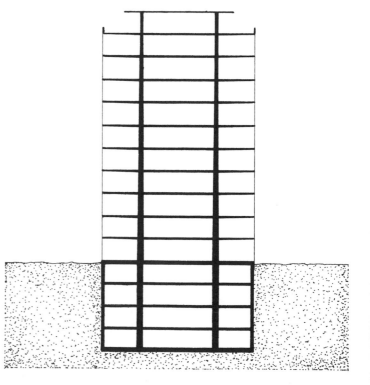

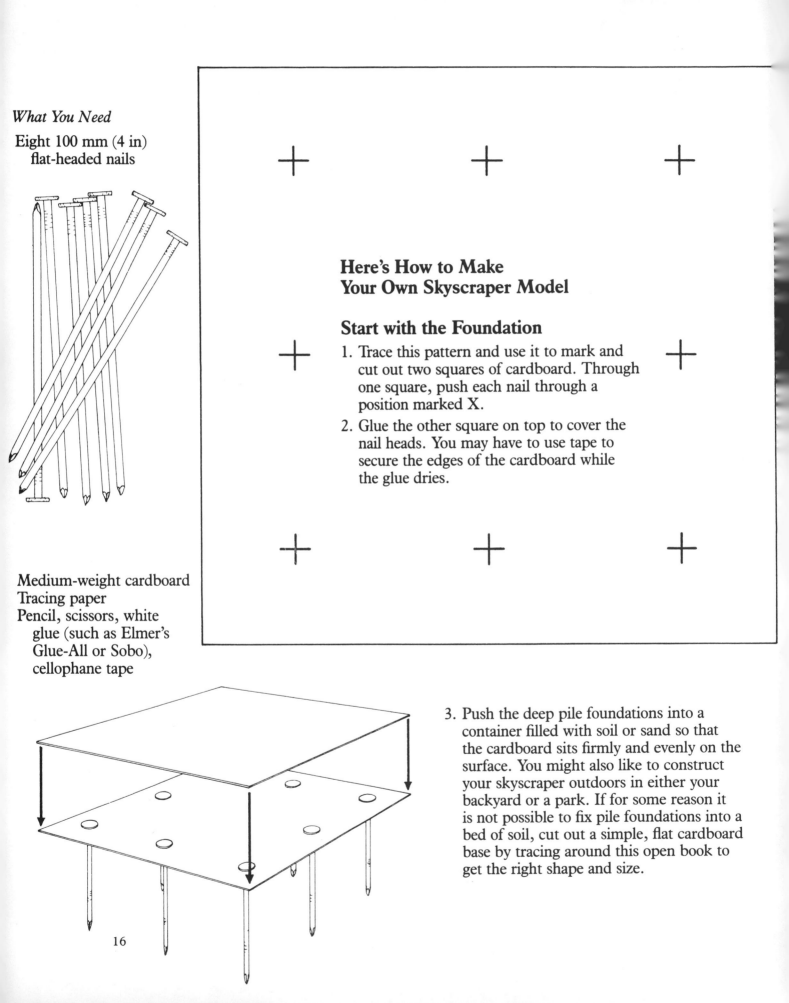

Eight 100 mm (4 in)
   flat-headed nails

Medium-weight cardboard
Tracing paper
Pencil, scissors, white
   glue (such as Elmer's
   Glue-All or Sobo),
   cellophane tape

Here's How to Make
Your Own Skyscraper Model

Start with the Foundation

1. Trace this pattern and use it to mark and
   cut out two squares of cardboard. Through
   one square, push each nail through a
   position marked X.

2. Glue the other square on top to cover the
   nail heads. You may have to use tape to
   secure the edges of the cardboard while
   the glue dries.

3. Push the deep pile foundations into a
   container filled with soil or sand so that
   the cardboard sits firmly and evenly on the
   surface. You might also like to construct
   your skyscraper outdoors in either your
   backyard or a park. If for some reason it
   is not possible to fix pile foundations into a
   bed of soil, cut out a simple, flat cardboard
   base by tracing around this open book to
   get the right shape and size.

16

III The Frame Goes Up

Load-bearing walls were used in early multistory buildings. In this type of construction, the walls support the weight of the building and carry its roof.

As buildings grew taller they also became heavier, and so their walls had to be made stronger. In the Middle Ages, the extra strength that was needed to support towers was provided by making walls thicker, especially at their base, where the greatest weight rested. The ground floors of these buildings were used only for entrances, so it didn't matter if the floor space in this area was reduced by the thickness of the walls.

Modern skyscrapers, however, were built to provide as much space as possible; therefore, it seemed that walls would have to be reduced in size. Apart from taking up too much space, though, load-bearing walls, no matter how thick, could not be made strong enough to support buildings once they reached a certain height and weight.

For these reasons, builders were forced to look for an alternative to load-bearing walls. Experiments with different construction ideas took time to develop until strong materials could also be found to help build skyscrapers safely. First iron and then steel was tried, and eventually use of these metals led to the invention of the *skeleton frame* and the first true skyscrapers.

The Change Begins

The changeover to the skeleton frame began in the late eighteenth century. Water-powered factories and textile mills rose five to seven stories in height in order for machinery to be close to the power source. Power was generated by large waterwheels, which themselves extended several stories in height. A typical mill of the late eighteenth century can be seen on the next page.

Mills had thick, load-bearing walls made of stone or brick; their floors were supported by wooden columns and beams. These early buildings, which contained highly flammable materials, were always in danger of fire. Wooden floors were saturated with oil that dripped from machinery, and candles and oil lamps were used for lighting. To reduce the risk, wood was replaced by cast and wrought iron.

There were many advantages to building with iron. For one thing, beams and columns could be made in the exact shapes and sizes required by the builder. This *standardization* of parts meant that buildings could be made more quickly and at less expense than ever before.

When steam engines were invented and first used in 1783, cast iron proved to be particularly useful. Iron could be easily molded into hollow columns, through which steam could travel to power equipment and heat factories. By this revolutionary development it became obvious that skeleton frames could be useful in more ways than one.

In the manufacture of iron products, the hot liquid metal is poured into molds. The result is cast iron, which is reasonably strong, though brittle, and when used for beams or columns it can snap easily.

Cast iron when hammered produces a much stronger metal, which we know as wrought iron. However, the extra labor and expense involved in making wrought iron limited its use to ties and connecting pieces for cast-iron columns and beams. Used in this way, wrought iron's strength could make up for cast iron's weaknesses.

Iron in either form, however, is badly affected by heat. To protect it from the extreme heat produced by machinery, and in the event of fire, brick and concrete were introduced. Iron beams were placed on iron columns, and the spaces in between were filled with flat brick arches to form the floors. These floors were then covered with a layer of concrete, a material that was versatile, lightweight, and fireproof. Together, this combination of materials proved to be a great step forward for multistory building.

The First Skyscrapers

Steel proved to be an ideal material for skyscrapers, or cloudscrapers as they were first known. It was lightweight, stronger than iron, and flexible, and therefore easy to work with. It had all the right qualities needed to produce really big buildings that were both strong and safe.

In 1854 a British inventor, Henry Bessemer, discovered a way of changing large quantities of iron into steel. German inventor Karl von Siemens and his French colleague, Pierre Émile Martin, developed a highly efficient steel-making furnace at about the same time. The names of these inventors may sound familiar because their methods and machines are still in use and form the basis of today's steel industry.

The problem of turning first iron, and then steel, into useful shapes and sizes was solved by the development of *rolling mills*, machines with rotating rollers that produced standard-size beams, columns, and other building parts. The electric motor was invented during that period, and its use in powering rolling mills made the mass production of steel products possible.

The first true skyscraper was built in Chicago in 1884 by William Le Baron Jenney. This 10-story building, designed for the Home Insurance Company of New York, had a self-supporting skeleton frame. For the first six stories cast-iron columns were bolted to wrought-iron I-shaped beams. When the frame reached this level, however, Jenney learned that the Carnegie-Phipps Steel Company was making Bessemer steel beams at their factory in Pittsburgh.

Steel had already earned itself a good reputation in bridge, railway, and ship building, and Jenney was anxious to experiment with it in his skyscraper. He did this by using steel beams instead of iron beams in the four remaining floors of the frame. Though steel was not a new material, it was treated as such because this was the first time it had been used in multi-story buildings. The results of Jenney's experiments were so good that skyscraper frames have been made of steel ever since.

21

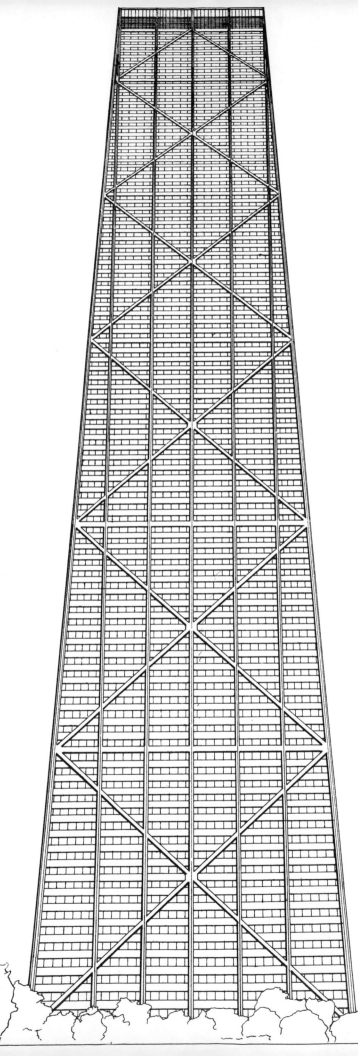

The Skeleton Frame

The job of a skeleton frame is to carry a skyscraper's weight. This weight is referred to as the *load*. The load includes the actual weight of the building: its foundation, frame, floors, roof, walls, and all the trims and furnishings that are likely to be brought into the building.

The movement of air around tall buildings is also taken into consideration in measuring loads. Enormous building surfaces are exposed to continually changing air movement. At great heights the speed of air increases, and the force of such winds adds a considerable weight to the overall load of the building.

Just as wind sways a tree, strong winds at great heights can cause unsafe movement in a skyscraper. For this reason, a skyscraper's frame must be strong and rigid. To make a frame stiff enough to withstand wind pressure, *bracing* is sometimes used on the outside surfaces of the building.

Skidmore, Owings and Merrill designed the 100-story, 337m (1107 ft) John Hancock Tower in Chicago (at left), in which a dozen pairs of braced tubes were used as stiffening.

The Core

The core acts like a spine to the skeleton frame. It is the skyscraper's main source of strength and at the same time the center for vital services, such as elevators, stairways, power supply, plumbing, and air conditioning.

The core is a hollow, reinforced concrete tube situated at the center of the skyscraper. Reinforced concrete is fireproof, so this serves as good protection for stairs and elevators; however, the most important quality of reinforced concrete is its ability to withstand all stresses experienced by a skyscraper. Steel is strong when it is stretched (*tension*) by weight or other forces that may pull at it. Concrete is strong when it is pressed together (*compression*). Neither material is strong enough on its own to cope with forces of both tension and compression, but together concrete and steel are unbeatable.

The design of the National Westminster Tower in London makes good use of the core as an obvious part of its design. The 183m (600 ft) tower, designed by R. Seifert and Partners, is the tallest *cantilevered* building in the world. Its floors extend out from the core, and the core supports the floors by acting as a counterweight. The thickness of the core's reinforced concrete varies at different levels to provide the support required at each point. For example, at its base the core's walls are 1,500mm (5 ft) thick; at its middle, 800mm (2.5 ft) thick; and at its top, the 52nd floor, only 120mm (5 in) thick. Interestingly, and for the same reasons, there is a similarity in shape between the modern skyscraper's core and the defensive towers of the Middle Ages as seen on page 12.

Building the Core

What You Need

Medium-weight cardboard
Tracing paper
Pencil, scissors or X-acto knife, ruler,
   white glue

1. Cut out a piece of cardboard 305mm
   (12 in) wide and 520mm (20.5 in) long.

2. Draw three lines on the pattern 75mm
   (3 in) apart and from both sides as shown.

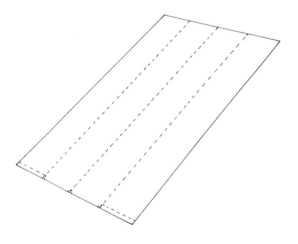

3. Illustration A shows the actual size of
   the ground floor of the core and half of
   the second floor. Using this as a guide
   and starting from the bottom of your
   cardboard pattern, mark off five stories
   and elevator openings, one above the
   other, including the flaps on the ground
   floor only (see right). These will be used
   later to secure the core to the foundation.

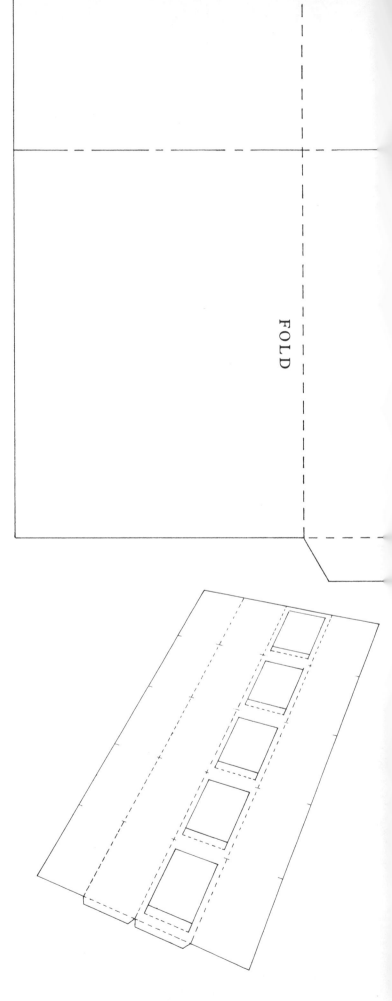

FOLD

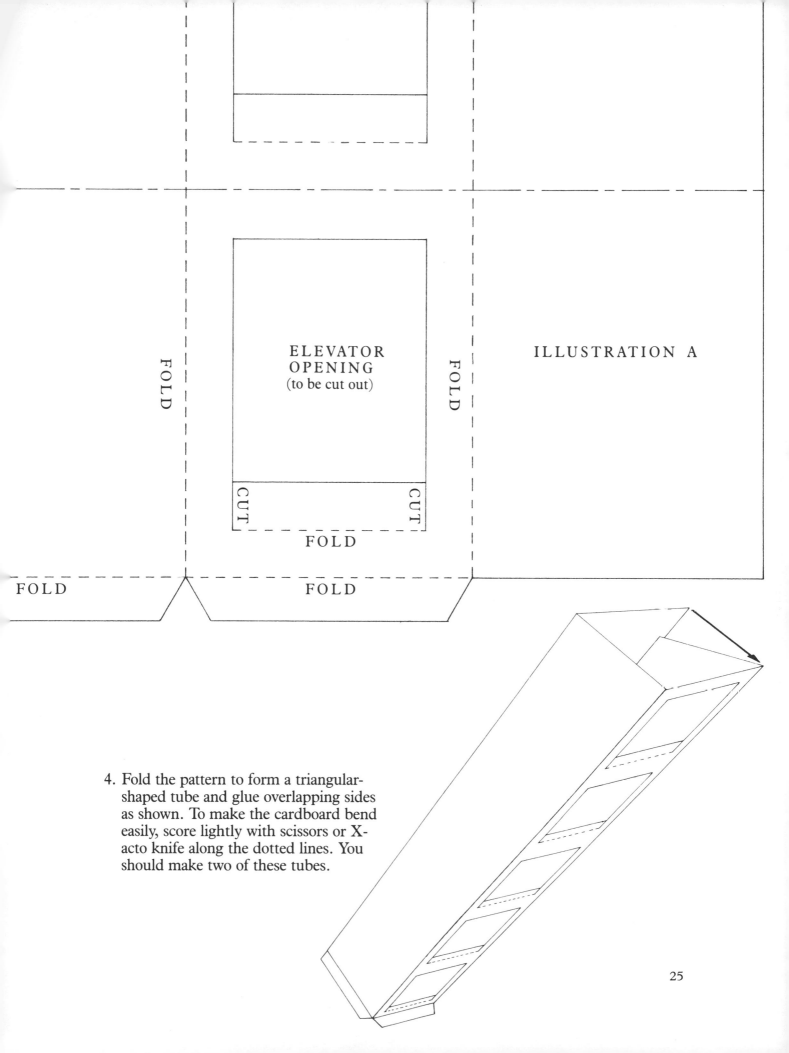

FOLD

ELEVATOR
OPENING
(to be cut out)

FOLD

ILLUSTRATION A

CUT

CUT

FOLD

FOLD

FOLD

FOLD

4. Fold the pattern to form a triangular-shaped tube and glue overlapping sides as shown. To make the cardboard bend easily, score lightly with scissors or X-acto knife along the dotted lines. You should make two of these tubes.

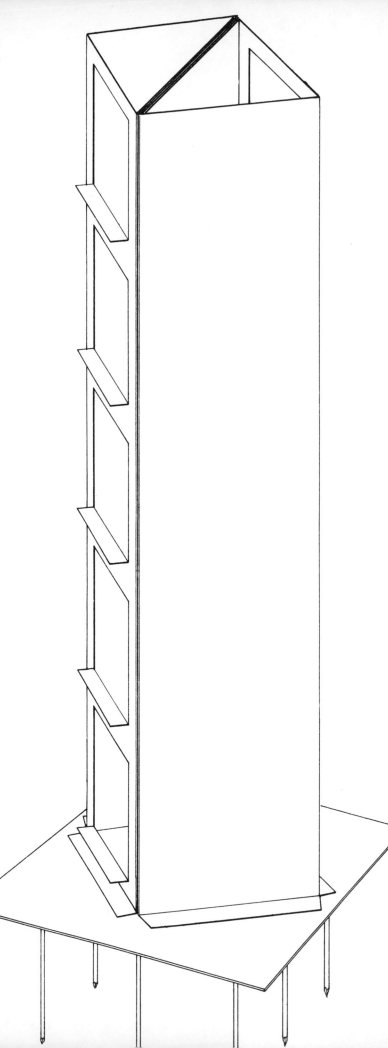

5. Glue the tubes together, placing the thicker, overlapped sides against each other. The thickness of the cardboard will make the core stiff and strong enough to support the skyscraper's floors, roof, and walls.

6. Fold out the four flaps at the core's base and glue these to the foundation.

7. Fold out and crease the flaps under each elevator opening. These flaps will later be used to support the floors.

IV Services That Make Skyscrapers Work

Air conditioning, electricity, plumbing, telecommunications, vertical transportation, and fire-safety systems–these are some of the services that keep a skyscraper running like an enormous machine, twenty-four hours a day. These services create a comfortable, healthy place to live and work; without any one of them, skyscrapers would not be practical.

Vertical Transportation

While the use of steel in the skeleton frame led to the development of skyscrapers, the invention of safe vertical transportation–that is, elevators–was equally important, because until that time buildings had to be limited to about six stories, which was as far as people could climb or carry goods.

Elevators of one sort or another have been in use for centuries. The earliest were described by Vitruvius, a Roman architect-engineer in the first century B.C.; however, the elevator that could carry passengers in safety was not invented until 1853.

Elisha Graves Otis, an American mechanic who worked in a bed factory, discovered a way to prevent freight elevators from falling if the ropes holding them were to break.

Using a steel wagon spring, Otis invented a safety brake that would stop the platform or car by gripping the elevator's guide rails. This simple yet highly efficient system was demonstrated by Mr. Otis at the Crystal Palace Exhibition in New York in 1854. Enclosed passenger cars were designed soon thereafter for use in multistory buildings. The first of these was installed in the Haughwout Building, a department store in New York; and by 1872 more than two thousand elevators were in service. Today the company Otis founded, only one of many supplying elevators, installs between 20,000 and 25,000 elevators (and escalators) every year.

Elevators no longer use steel wagon springs, but the principle that makes them safe is just the same. Though the design has certainly changed since 1854, the differences have to do with the buildings they are in. The changing styles and sizes of skyscrapers, which affected the design of elevators, is best seen on New York's skyline, pictured on the next pages.

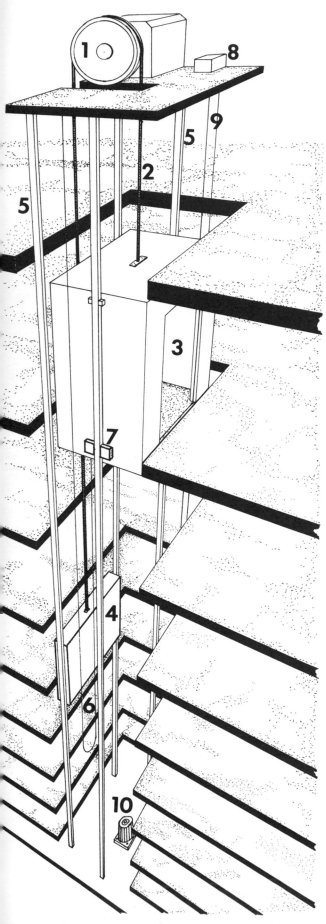

How Elevators Work

Modern elevators work in the same way that the earliest hoists did–that is, by pulling two approximately equal weights over a wheel. Moving up and down, each weight counterbalances the other, and in so doing causes the wheel to turn. In a modern elevator:

(1) the electric motor turns a grooved wheel, or *drive sheave*, that pulls:

(2) the *hoist ropes*. These are connected to and hold:

(3) the *cab*, or *car*, and:

(4) the *counterweight*. It works together with the motor to pull the car up and down. The counterweight counterbalances the car, as both are approximately the same weight. Both the car and the counterweight have:

(5) *guide rails*, which are like railroad tracks. In this case they keep the car and the counterweight steady.

(6) *Traveling cables* are power lines that carry power from the motor to the car to operate doors, lighting, and air conditioning in the car itself.

(7) *Safeties* are wedges on the car that act like brakes, operating if the car moves too quickly. If the safeties do not work:

(8) the *governor*, like Otis's wagon spring, grips:

(9) the *governor cable*, clamping against the car's guide rails and bringing it to a gradual, safe stop.

(10) The *buffer* sits at the bottom on the elevator shaft to prevent the car from falling into the pit should all other safety devices fail. It is a kind of cushion for the car.

New Elevator Designs

Until recently, the height of skyscrapers has been limited because the number of elevators required to service them took up too much space. More space means more income from rentals, and if elevators took up space that would otherwise be rented, income would be reduced and skyscrapers would become uneconomical.

To overcome the space problem, Otis designed the *Skylobby* system, which may be seen in this cross section of the World Trade Center.

These two towers, which are the tallest buildings on New York City's skyline, have the largest vertical transportation system in the world. Each 410m (1,350 ft) and 110 stories high, the towers are served by 238 elevators and 74 escalators. Approximately fifty thousand people work in these buildings and another eighty thousand people visit each day. Having a population equal to that of a medium-sized city, the twin towers needed an efficient elevator system that didn't take up too much room.

The Skylobby system treats each tower as though it were three separate buildings stacked on top of each other. While a number of elevators travel from the fifth basement below ground to the 108th floor, the rest are divided up in this way: the ground floor to the 44th floor; the 44th floor to the 78th floor; and the 78th floor to the top.

Space has been allowed for machine rooms above each group of elevators. These rooms are fitted with ventilating equipment that keeps the machinery cool. In addition to getting very hot, elevator motors are also very noisy. As the machine rooms are isolated, the noise does not disturb anyone.

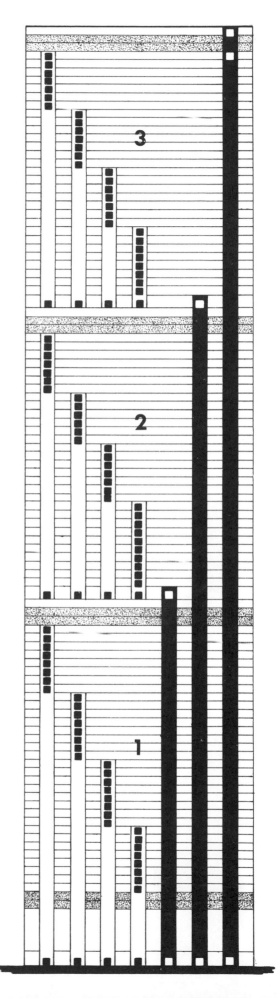

Making a Movable Elevator

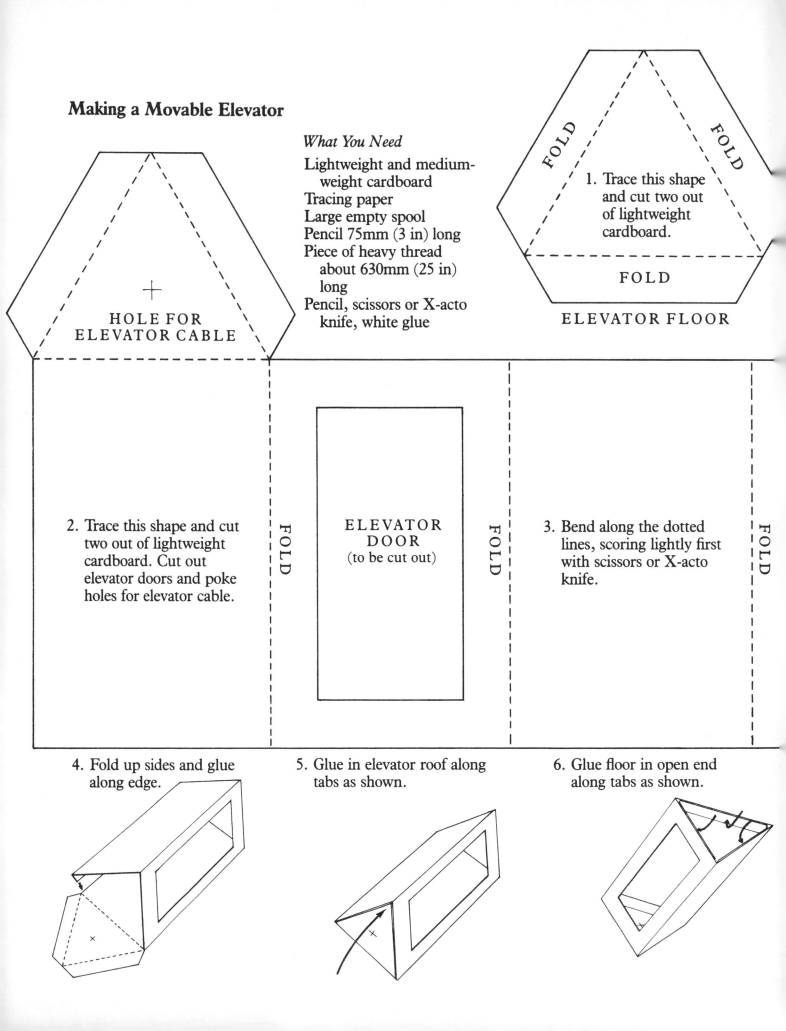

What You Need

Lightweight and medium-weight cardboard
Tracing paper
Large empty spool
Pencil 75mm (3 in) long
Piece of heavy thread about 630mm (25 in) long
Pencil, scissors or X-acto knife, white glue

+

HOLE FOR
ELEVATOR CABLE

FOLD

FOLD

FOLD

1. Trace this shape and cut two out of lightweight cardboard.

ELEVATOR FLOOR

2. Trace this shape and cut two out of lightweight cardboard. Cut out elevator doors and poke holes for elevator cable.

FOLD

ELEVATOR DOOR
(to be cut out)

FOLD

3. Bend along the dotted lines, scoring lightly first with scissors or X-acto knife.

FOLD

4. Fold up sides and glue along edge.

5. Glue in elevator roof along tabs as shown.

6. Glue floor in open end along tabs as shown.

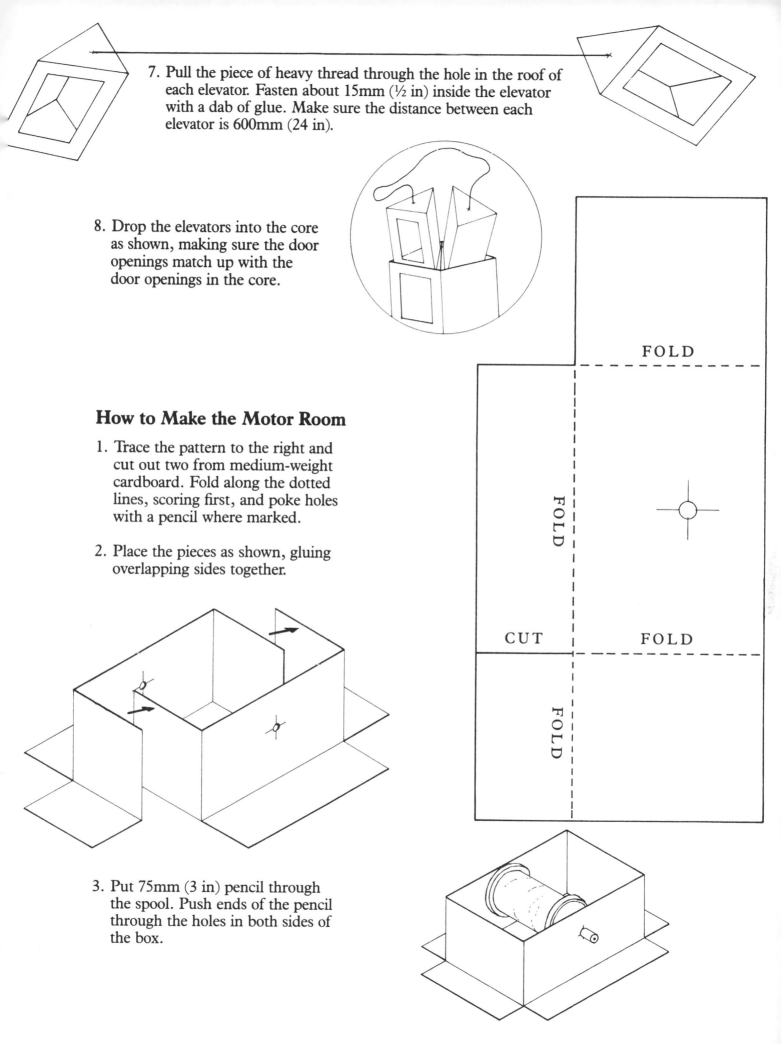

7. Pull the piece of heavy thread through the hole in the roof of each elevator. Fasten about 15mm (½ in) inside the elevator with a dab of glue. Make sure the distance between each elevator is 600mm (24 in).

8. Drop the elevators into the core as shown, making sure the door openings match up with the door openings in the core.

How to Make the Motor Room

1. Trace the pattern to the right and cut out two from medium-weight cardboard. Fold along the dotted lines, scoring first, and poke holes with a pencil where marked.

2. Place the pieces as shown, gluing overlapping sides together.

3. Put 75mm (3 in) pencil through the spool. Push ends of the pencil through the holes in both sides of the box.

FOLD

FOLD

CUT   FOLD

FOLD

Services Are Centrally Located

The services that keep a skyscraper running are centrally placed in the building's core. This is the most convenient location, since grouping services together saves valuable floor space. It is also the most economical position, since less pipe, wiring, and so on is used when services are placed directly over each other on each floor. This is also the safest place for services, since they are protected by the concrete core, which is fireproof.

To understand the way these services fit into the core's plan, it is best to look down into the roof of a skyscraper. Pictured below is a typical floor plan, which shows the different services. While this plan shows only one floor's design, it represents all floors, which are exactly the same.

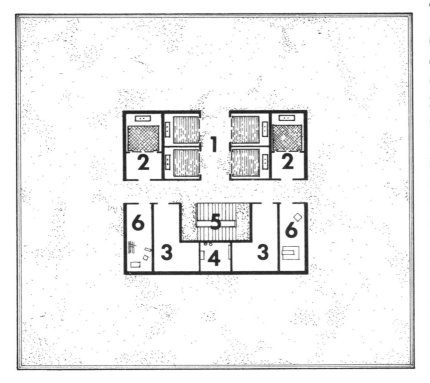

The services are:

(1) passenger elevators
(2) freight and fire elevators
(3) toilets
(4) electrical and mechanical services
(5) stairs
(6) storage areas.

The remaining space is designed on what has been called an *open plan*, because there are no walls dividing the open space into individual offices.

Floors and Ceilings Serve a Useful Purpose

At the end of the nineteenth century very little effort was made to hide pipes and wiring even though they sometimes spoiled a skyscraper's appearance. The benefit of having services in full view, however, was to make it easier to carry out regular maintenance and to locate and repair faults and problems. As services increased in size and number according to the growing needs of taller buildings, they were hidden for appearance, public safety, and relief from the heat.

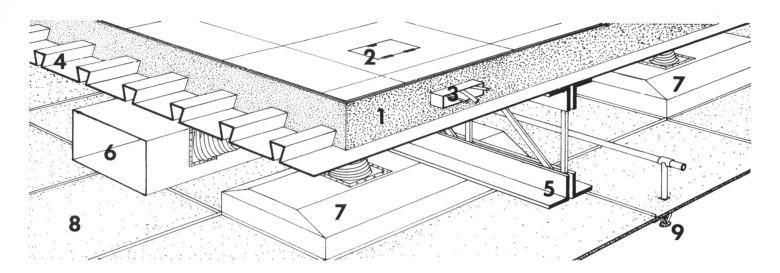

Today, services are carried from the core through floors and ceilings to wherever they may be needed. This way they are accessible for maintenance and of the least inconvenience in open-plan offices.

(1) The fireproof layer of concrete on which carpeting and tiles may be laid.

(2) Telephone and electricity outlets set in the concrete and covered by protective metal flaps. No matter how often furniture is rearranged in open-plan offices, outlets will still be within easy reach.

(3) Steel ducts, sometimes cast in concrete, carry telephone cables and electrical wiring.

(4) Steel decking supports the floor and may be part of the skeleton frame.

(5) Steel floor trusses are fixed to the frame and act as the floor's main support. I-shaped steel beams may also be used for this purpose.

(6) Air conditioning ducts carry both warm and cool air through the building.

(7) Air-conditioning ducts are next to lighting fixtures so that the heat produced by the lights may be pulled back into this system to be used for heating elsewhere.

(8) Ceilings are suspended from floor trusses or beams. They are made of a fireproof material that absorbs sound.

(9) Fire alarms and sprinkler systems are spaced evenly apart to cover the greatest area. They react to smoke and excessive heat. Alarms sound the warning, and sprinklers release water to assist in putting out fires.

Note: Today, floor units are *prefabricated*–that is, made in a factory and installed as a complete unit. This method of construction saves builders time and money.

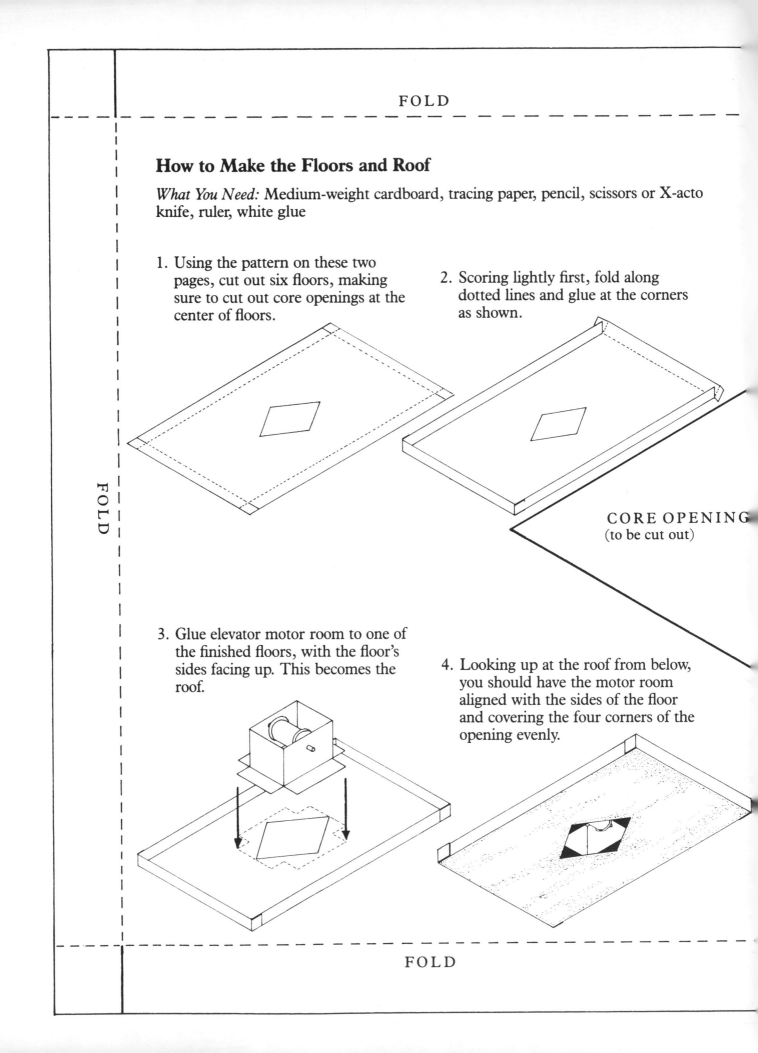

How to Make the Floors and Roof

What You Need: Medium-weight cardboard, tracing paper, pencil, scissors or X-acto knife, ruler, white glue

1. Using the pattern on these two pages, cut out six floors, making sure to cut out core openings at the center of floors.

2. Scoring lightly first, fold along dotted lines and glue at the corners as shown.

CORE OPENING
(to be cut out)

3. Glue elevator motor room to one of the finished floors, with the floor's sides facing up. This becomes the roof.

4. Looking up at the roof from below, you should have the motor room aligned with the sides of the floor and covering the four corners of the opening evenly.

5. Push each floor over the core, fixing it in place by resting it on the flaps at the bottom of each elevator opening.

6. Place the roof at the top of the model. Glue in place around the top edge of the core. Remove the pencil and spool from the motor room and wrap the thread, which acts like the elevator cable, twice around the spool. The elevator is now properly suspended and may be moved up and down by turning the spool. The two elevators, equal in weight, counterbalance each other, operating in the same way as a real elevator and its counterweight do.

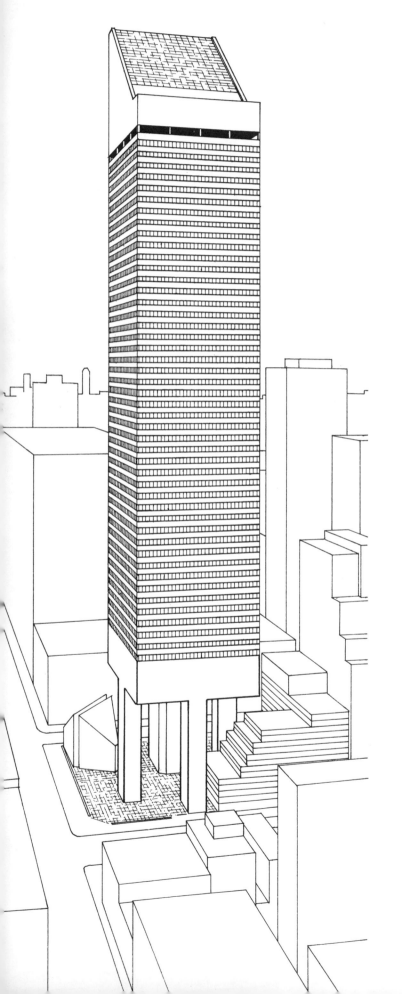

Looking to the Future

Services in the 279m (915 ft) Citicorp Center in New York are operated by computers—two of them, in fact. If one computer fails, the other is there to take over automatically. This highly sophisticated system, called *Building Management System* (BMS), supervises and controls heating, ventilation, air conditioning, and lights at 2200 points throughout the 59-story tower. Once every minute the computer checks the temperature at most of these points, adjusting services as may be required.

Also within the system's care are twenty double-decker elevators and a security system that keeps an eye on twelve hundred spots in the building with the help of closed-circuit television.

Under the tower's sloping roof is the *Tuned Mass Damper*, which works on a principle that is not as complicated as it sounds. A four-hundred-ton block of concrete, floating on a pool of oil, is moved from side to side when the BMS registers the building's sway at more than half a meter (1.6 ft) per second. By counterbalancing, or moving in the opposite direction to the wind, the building's movement in winds as strong as 200kph (125 mph) can be reduced by almost half.

V Walls and Windows for Protection and Personality

Early multistory buildings such as the Roman insulae and fortified towers had thick, load-bearing walls. They were built of standard-size clay bricks and stone blocks that were easy to handle, as well as being stronger than other materials available at the time.

The invention of the self-supporting skeleton frame toward the end of the nineteenth century meant that walls, no longer needed for support, didn't have to be so thick, or their window openings so small.

In the modern skyscraper, the main function of the walls is to provide protection from the weather, and to do this job, walls have to be able to withstand strong winds at great heights, as well as transfer their own weight, plus the added weight from strong winds, evenly over the skeleton frame to which they are attached.

Walls that entirely cover the skeleton frame are called *cladding*. They hide the building's frame from view, acting very much like a curtain, which is where the term *curtain wall* comes from.

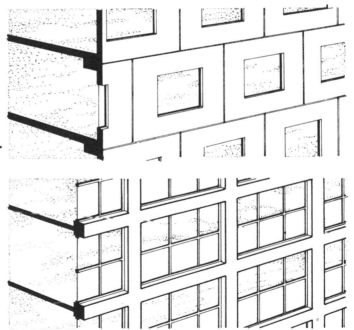

Walls that fit between the frame are known as *infill panels*–that is, they fill in the empty spaces left by the columns and beams, using the frame as part of the overall decoration.

With the invention of mechanical lifting devices, wall construction has become fast and efficient. Cladding and infill panels, manufactured as complete units in a factory, can be hoisted into place and fixed to the frame in no time at all, and when in place they give a skyscraper a character and personality all its own.

The great fire that destroyed many of the buildings in Chicago in 1870 provided a great opportunity for large-scale redevelopment of this American city. Business and commercial buildings took the form of skyscrapers because they provided so much office space on a small amount of land. William Le Baron Jenney opened the way for skyscraper development with the invention of the skeleton frame, as described on page 20. Following in Jenney's footsteps, The Chicago School, a group of architects living in the right city at the right time, was to become responsible for many skyscrapers and the revolutionary development that has become known as the *Chicago window*.

Louis Sullivan, who designed the skyscrapers on these pages, was one of the School's greatest pioneers. On the facing page is his Wainwright Building, which was built in St. Louis, Missouri, in 1891. The walls were built using large bricks. The single windows placed in vertical rows exaggerate the height of the building, making it look taller.

The heavy appearance, with its great amount of decoration, was popular at that time because people wanted buildings to look like something out of the past, such as the classical temple buildings of Greece and Rome. Eight years later, however, Sullivan designed the Carson, Pirie, Scott department store in Chicago, which is pictured here. What makes this 12-story skyscraper look so different from the Wainwright Building is the limited use of decoration, and the new window design—the Chicago window. Stretching horizontally across the building, the new windows were made up of a large, fixed center pane of glass, with smaller windows on either side that could be opened for ventilation.

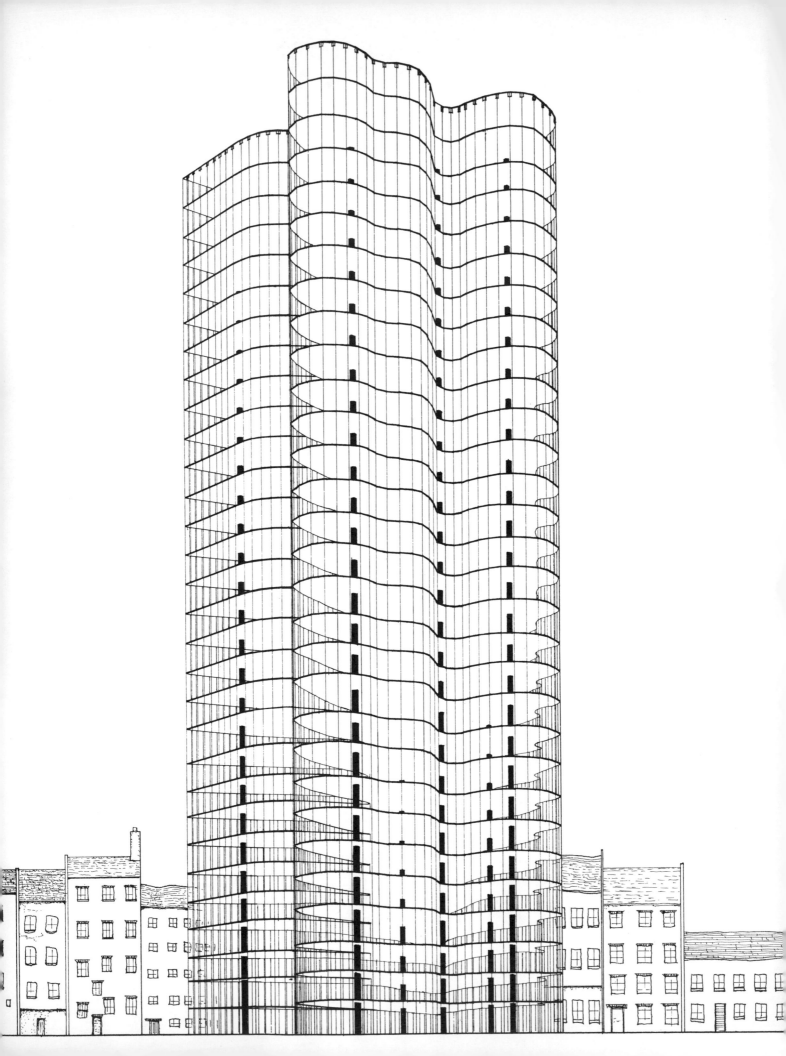

While America gave birth to the skyscraper, Europe dominated its design during the early twentieth century. During the 20s the German art school at Dessau, the *Bauhaus* (House of Building), did much to encourage all areas of the arts, including architecture, so that Germany became the center of creative genius during the years before World War II.

Swiss-born French architect Charles-Édouard Jeanneret, who became known as Le Corbusier (The Crow), went to Germany for inspiration. There he worked for a short time with leading German architect Peter Behrens. Le Corbusier is probably best remembered for his skyscrapers for living–huge apartment blocks that were copied throughout Europe and were particularly popular in Britain.

At the same time Mies Van der Rohe and Walter Gropius, two of the many architects associated with the Bauhaus, worked on ideas that have formed the basis for modern skyscraper design. On the facing page is a picture of a model for a 30-story glass skyscraper that Mies Van der Rohe submitted for a competition in 1921.

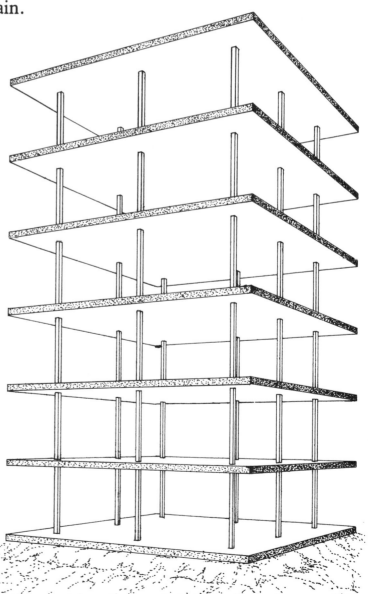

Cantilevered concrete floors project beyond the frame's columns. Covered by nothing more than a curtain of glass, the floors appear to be floating in air. The diagram on the right shows how this idea works. The development that began with Walter Gropius' early factory buildings in Germany has resulted in the removal of heavy corners on skyscrapers. Compare the Wainwright Building on page 40 with the buildings on the next pages.

New York's Lever House, designed by Gordon Bunschaft of Skidmore, Owings and Merrill, was completed in 1952. It was the first of many skyscrapers to be built in the style developed by the Bauhaus architects. Covered in green-tinted glass and stainless steel, the 24-story tower, shown at left, is supported by *pilotis*, which is a French term for stilts that raise a building one story to create an open space underneath.

Pilotis also support a low adjoining building, which on the ground floor has a patio-courtyard. There is a restaurant on the first floor and the roof has become a garden for the use and enjoyment of the building's workers.

Pictured to the right is Mies Van der Rohe's (with Philip Johnson) Seagram Building, also in New York, which was based on his earlier skyscraper designs. The 38-story tower, completed in 1958, is covered in bronze metal and smoky-colored glass. The rectangular-shaped building is set back from the road by almost 30.5m (100 ft). In such a crowded city as New York, the open space is as welcome a sight as the simply designed building itself.

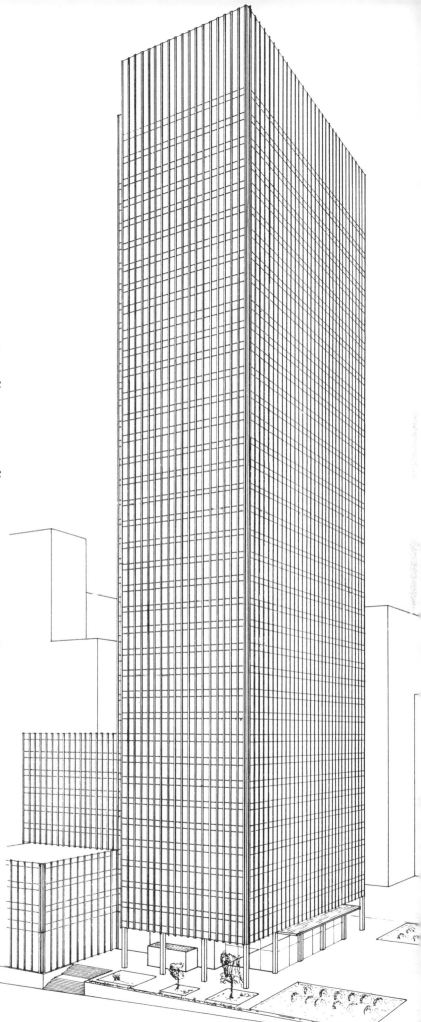

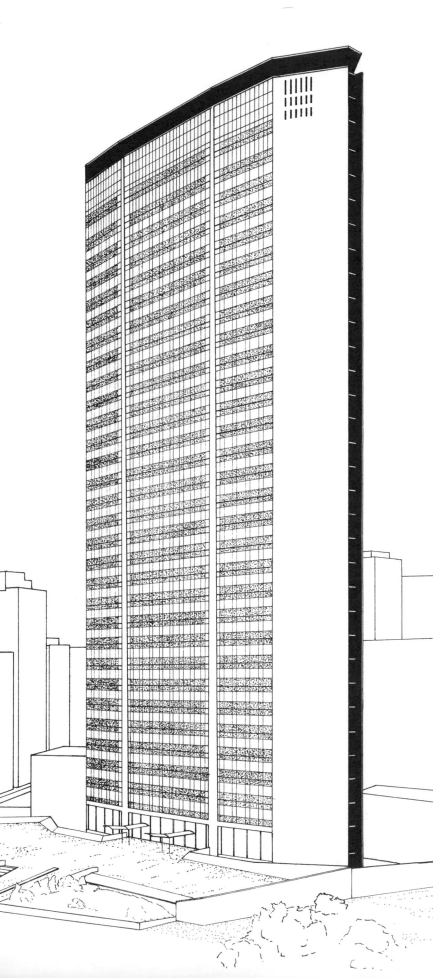

Interest in the glass curtain wall was replaced by the use of concrete at the end of the 1950s. Concrete-covered skyscrapers, such as the Pirelli Tower pictured here and the Pan American Building on the facing page, took on new shapes and different looks with a material that could be precast with a variety of smooth and textured surfaces. An added bonus with concrete was its ability to be reinforced, or prestressed, to add further stiffening to the structure. The Pirelli Tower in Milan was built in 1959 by Gio Ponti and Pier Luigi Nervi, while the Pan Am Building in New York, designed by Walter Gropius, was completed in 1963. Both buildings were made with quick-to-assemble, prefabricated concrete panels.

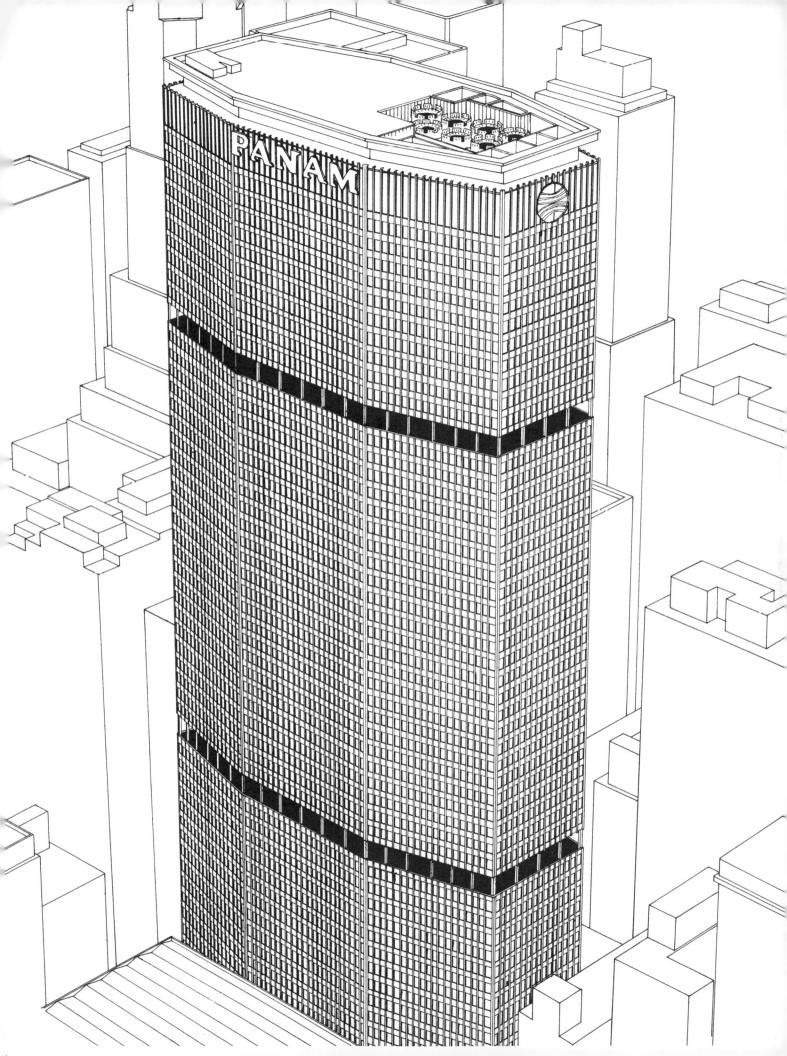

How to Make the Curtain Walls

What You Need: Lightweight cardboard, tracing paper, scissors or X-acto knife, pencil, ruler, white glue

1. Using the two patterns opposite, trace and cut out ten of each to form the curtain walls, or cladding.

2. Scoring lightly first, fold the top edge, making this fold as flat as possible.

3. Each wall panel is then hooked over the floor above, while its bottom edge is either tucked into the floor below or glued to the outside. The drawing below has part of the model cut away to show how the panels are fixed in place.

4. You can glue the curtain walls in place if you want to make the model more permanent, or you may leave them free so you can change the design of the walls from time to time.

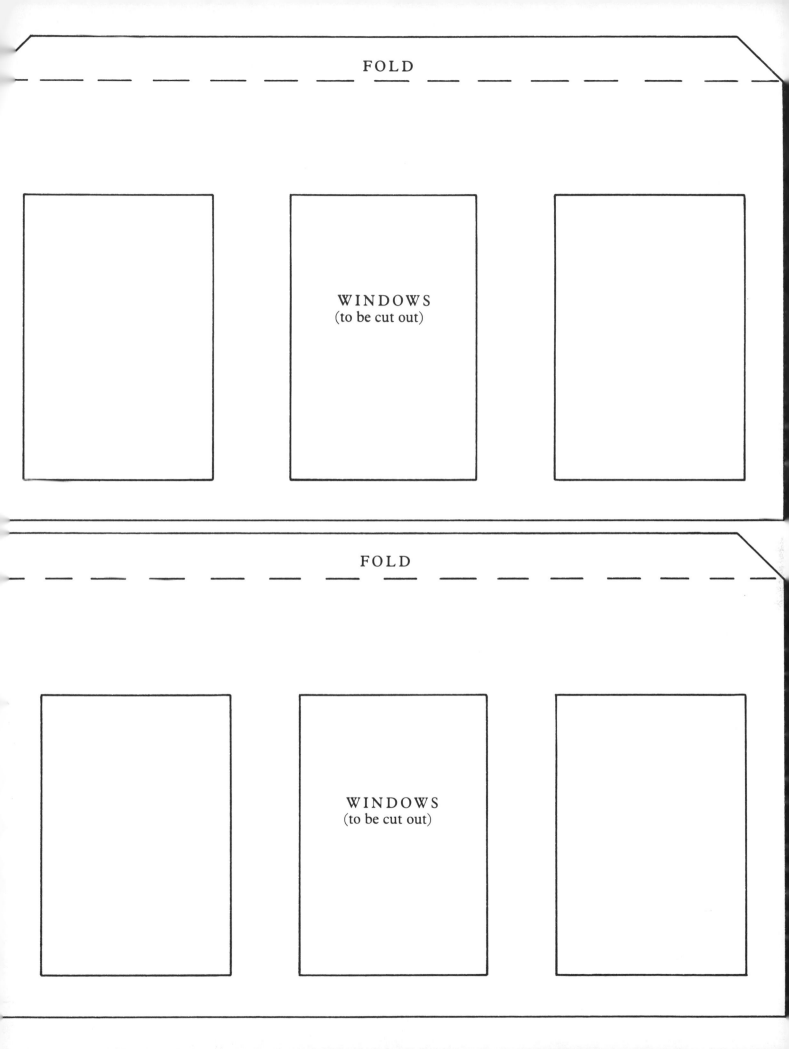

FOLD

WINDOWS
(to be cut out)

FOLD

WINDOWS
(to be cut out)

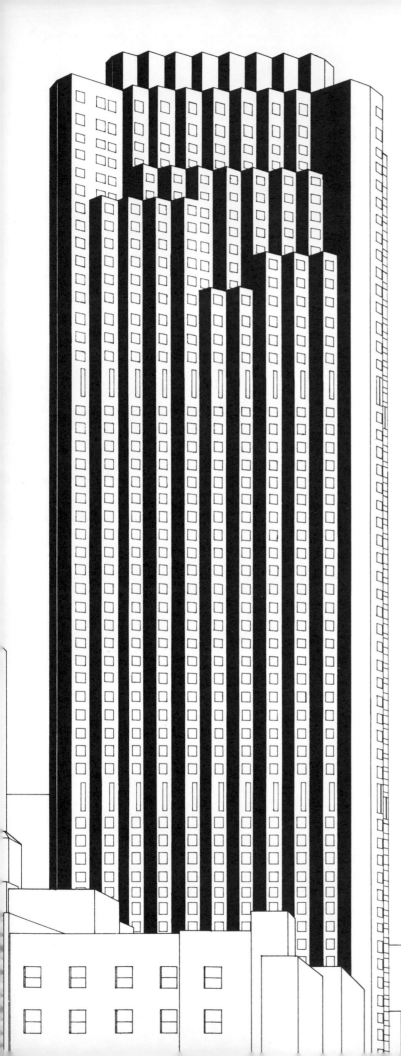

Finally, the 52-story headquarters for the Bank of America in San Francisco uses an old material in an interesting, new way. Rich, brown-colored granite stone, polished to a shine, has been used in zigzag walls that take their inspiration from the city's older architecture, with its much-loved bay windows. Designed by Wurster, Bernardi and Eammons Inc. (with Skidmore, Owings and Merrill and Pietro Belluschi) and completed in 1970, the world's biggest bank combines the best features and materials from the past and the present to produce a really grand building with a personality all its own.

VI Getting It All Together

When skyscrapers were first thought of, many of the problems associated with putting them together were solved by using traditional building methods. When skyscrapers reached thirty, forty, fifty, and one hundred stories, however, a separate industry, making prefabricated material, was needed to design equipment that would help to build and maintain them.

Also, at the lower heights of the early skeleton frames, workmen could carry out their jobs with limited discomfort and danger, and building costs could be controlled. This situation too has changed in recent years.

The organization of trade unions in countries throughout the world has led to the establishment of codes of practice that further limit the dangers and insure a minimum standard of comfort for workers. The rising cost of labor and building materials as well has meant that new systems have had to be found to make building safer and more efficient in terms of time and money.

Now, many of the jobs formerly done by workers on a building site are done miles away in a factory. Wall panels and floor and ceiling units are prefabricated in a factory, transported to a building site on vehicles specially designed for their carriage, and lifted into place with specially designed hoists.

The standardization of building parts has also contributed to the mass production of skyscrapers, since there need be no guesswork and time-consuming measuring and fitting when building parts are of a uniform size.

In the last century the building industry has developed a successful formula for putting skyscrapers together. The result is bigger and better skyscrapers, built in less time and at a cost that developers can afford.

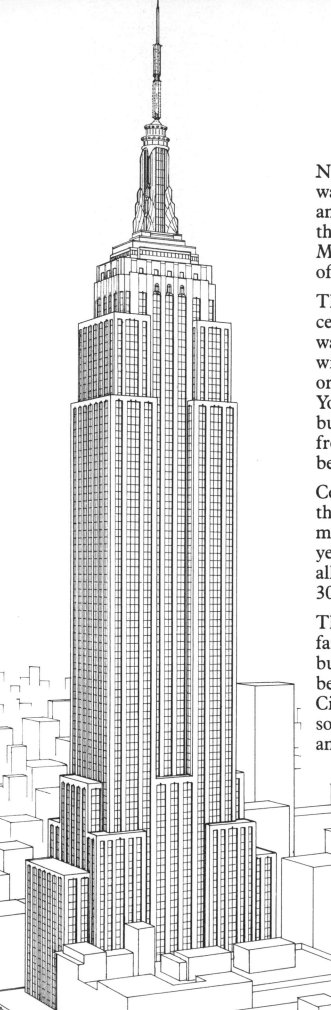

New York's Empire State Building was built in record-breaking time by anyone's standards. Construction of the steel-framed skyscraper began in May 1930 and progressed at an average of more than four stories a week.

The building's simple design, with a central, services core, featured *stepped* walls of Indiana limestone and granite, with stainless steel trim. The stepping, or setbacks, were required by New York City zoning laws so that tall buildings would not restrict daylight from entering into the narrow streets below.

Construction continued throughout the summer and the cold winter months, and by May 1931, just one year later, the Empire State Building, all 448m (1472 ft), 102 stories, and 303,000 tons of it, was completed.

The building that was to enjoy the fame of being the world's tallest building for forty years has since become the symbol of New York City–the Skyscraper City–and something of a challenge to architects and builders ever since.

The twin, 110-story World Trade Center towers in the same city was constructed by a quite different method. Skyscrapers like the Empire State Building have a framework that looks like a cage made with an almost equal number of columns and beams. In the Trade Center, however, there are fewer columns. Those that are used are in the core for stiffening, and on the outside edge of the tower, where they are tied together by steel beams encircling each floor like a giant belt. To give the structure its strength, trusses acting like beams are placed within the floor and ceiling areas to connect the core with the outside walls.

During the construction of the Trade Center, enormous *kangaroo cranes* were set up on the four corners of each core. These cranes were used to lift columns and beams as they were needed to complete each floor. When construction reached the height of the cranes, diesel-driven hydraulic jacks would lift them by jumping like a kangaroo, 3.6m (12 ft) each time. On completion of the World Trade Center, three cranes on each building were taken apart and lowered to the ground by the fourth. The fourth crane on each building was disassembled and removed by the freight elevator.

Lift-slab construction is yet another way of putting a skyscraper together. Cores are built, and at ground level an entire floor is assembled around them. When the floor, ceiling units, and outside walls have been completed, a hoist is used to lift them to the top of the core. Each story is done in the same way until the skyscraper, built from the top down, is finally finished.

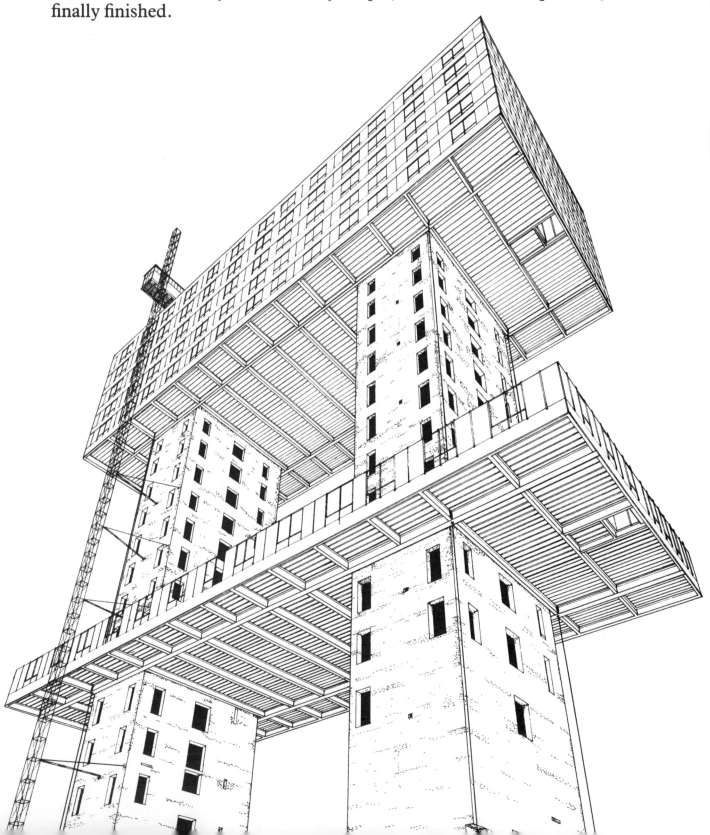

The Skyscraper Model

If you have followed all the steps in making the model, your skyscraper should look and work like the model pictured on page 55. If not, go back through the book and check each section: foundation, core, floors and roof, elevators, and cladding.

You can change the shape, size, color, and appearance of your model by varying the materials and designs you use. Instead of building a skyscraper with rectangular floors, design them in the shape of a circle, oval, or square. If you want square elevators, change the core design using two square-shaped tubes. Windows may be square, rectangular, circular, or any shape that takes your fancy. By changing these elements around and putting them together in different combinations, you will soon realize that anything and everything is possible with your model. Just as anything and everything is possible with a real skyscraper!